THE
PETER RABBIT
AND
FRIENDS
COOK BOOK ™

FREDERICK WARNE

Published by the Penguin Group
27 Wrights Lane, London W8 5TZ, England
Penguin Books USA Inc., 375 Hudson Street, New York, N.Y. 10014, USA
Penguin Books Australia Ltd, Ringwood, Victoria, Australia
Penguin Books Canada Ltd, 10 Alcorn Avenue, Toronto, Ontario, Canada M4V 3B2
Penguin Books (N.Z.) Ltd, 182-190 Wairau Road, Auckland 10, New Zealand

Penguin Books Ltd, Registered Offices: Harmondsworth, Middlesex, England

First published 1994
1 3 5 7 9 10 8 6 4 2
ISBN 0 7232 4146 5

Printed and bound in Great Britain by
William Clowes Limited, London and Beccles

THE
PETER RABBIT
AND FRIENDS
COOK BOOK ™

Written by Naia Bray-Moffatt

Illustrations from the authorized animated series
based on the original tales by

BEATRIX POTTER ™

F. WARNE & Co

CONTENTS

LUCIE'S COOKING RULES

1. It's always a good idea to wear an apron when you're cooking so that you don't get your clothes dirty. Even Mrs. Tiggy-winkle can't get some foodstains out of clothes.

2. Make sure that everything you are going to use for cooking is clean, and wash your hands before you start.

3. Cooking is fun, but you have to be careful too. Sharp knives can cut you and cookers can burn you, so always ask an adult to help. If you are using the oven or touching anything hot, always wear oven gloves and if you're cooking on a stove make sure that saucepan handles aren't sticking out so that you don't knock into them.

4. Read each recipe through carefully so you know what you need before you start cooking. It's very annoying to start cooking something and then find you haven't got an important ingredient. It's much quicker, too, if you have all the things you need ready to use before you start.

5. When you've finished cooking (or while you're waiting for something to cook) you have to wash up. The best way to wash up is to do the glass things first when the water is cleanest and then plates and lastly saucepans, knives and forks and the really dirty things. Be careful when you're washing knives not to cut yourself.

6. Enjoy cooking, and eating what you've made!

INTRODUCING LUCIE . . .

Once upon a time there was a little girl called Lucie, who lived on a farm. She was a good little girl but she was always losing things.

One day she came into the farmyard crying because she'd lost her apron. She asked all the animals in the farmyard if they'd seen it but none of them had.

'Oh dear,' cried Lucie, 'I specially need my apron because I want to have a party for Peter Rabbit and bake him a cake. I wonder if Mrs Tiggy-winkle has seen it. The last time I lost my handkerchiefs and my pinny she found them and washed them for me.'

So Lucie scrambled up the hill behind the farm to the house of Mrs Tiggy-winkle, the washerwoman. She knocked on a tiny door which went into the hillside and she walked into the farmhouse kitchen where a very stout, short person was busy washing and ironing.

'Oh, Mrs Tiggy-winkle, have you seen my apron? I want to have a party for Peter Rabbit and I need to wear my apron to do the cooking.'

Mrs Tiggy-winkle made a bob-curtsey. 'Oh, yes, if you please'm, it's here in the clothes basket.' And she ironed it and folded it and gave it to Lucie.

'Oh, that *is* lovely! Now I can do lots of cooking for the party. But Peter Rabbit has so many friends and they all like different things to eat. Will you help me plan what to cook, Mrs Tiggy-winkle?'

Mrs Tiggy-winkle's nose went sniffle, sniffle, snuffle and her eyes twinkled. 'If you please'm, Mrs Rabbit says the baker through the wood has a very good recipe for currant buns. She bought some the other day. He calls them currant bunnies, so Peter and his sisters, Flopsy, Mopsy, and Cotton-tail like them.'

Lucie took out a pencil and paper and wrote down:

MRS RABBIT'S CURRANT BUNS

What goes in them
– for 10 buns
8 oz (200 g) plain flour
pinch of salt
1 oz (25 g) margarine or butter
2 oz (50 g) sugar
2 oz (50 g) currants
1 packet easy blend dry yeast
1 egg
1 tbsp warm milk

How to make

1. Sieve the flour and salt into a large bowl.

2. Cut the margarine into small pieces and rub it into the flour with your fingertips until it looks like fine breadcrumbs.

3. Add the sugar, currants and packet of yeast and mix these in.

4. Crack the egg into a separate bowl (if any eggshell gets in by

mistake fish it out with a spoon). Add the milk and whisk with the eggs using a fork or a balloon whisk.

5. Pour the beaten egg mixture into the flour and stir well with a wooden spoon.

6. Cover the bowl with a clean tea-towel and leave in a warm place such as an airing cupboard, for an hour or until the mixture has about doubled in size. (While you're waiting for the dough to rise is a good time to do some washing up).

7. The dough should now be quite stretchy. Put it onto a floured surface and knead it by pulling half of the dough towards you and then pushing it back into the other half (Mrs Tiggy-winkle says it's a bit like washing clothes), and continue stretching and pulling different bits for a couple of minutes. Put the tea-towel back on top and leave for another 15 minutes.

8. Turn the oven on to 425°F/220°C/gas mark 7.

9. Cover a baking sheet with greaseproof paper and rub a tiny bit of margarine over it. Then divide the dough into 10 round shapes and put on the baking sheet at least 5 cms (2 inches) apart so they have room to spread.

10. Bake in the oven for about 15 minutes till the buns are brown. When they are ready, take them out of the oven and put on a wire rack to cool.

'Peter likes vegetables, too, doesn't he?' said Lucie. 'Mr McGregor has lots of vegetables in his garden – or at least he did until Peter ate them all. I could chop up some salad vegetables like carrots, radishes, celery and cucumber and make things to dip them into.' Lucie began to write again:

LUCIE'S DIPS FOR PETER RABBIT'S FAVOURITE VEGETABLES

AVOCADO DIP
What goes in it
1 ripe avocado
1 dsp natural yoghurt
1 dsp mayonnaise
squeeze of lemon juice
salt and pepper

How to make

1. Cut the avocado in half and remove the stone in the middle.
2. Scoop out the avocado from the skin and mash in a bowl with a fork until it's smooth and creamy.

3. Add all the other ingredients and mix in well. Taste it to see if it needs any more salt or pepper.

CUCUMBER DIP

What goes in it

1 cucumber
4 mint sprigs
1 clove of garlic
10 oz (250 g) natural yoghurt
1 tsp white wine vinegar

How to make

1. Peel the cucumber with a vegetable peeler and chop into cubes of about 5 mm ($^1/_4$ inch) square. Put them into a bowl.
2. Wash the mint sprigs, chop into little pieces and add to the cucumber.
3. Peel the garlic clove, press in a garlic press and add to the cucumber.
4. Add the yoghurt and vinegar and stir all the ingredients together.
5. Put in the fridge for about half an hour before you want to eat it so that all the flavours come out.

COTTAGE CHEESE DIP

What goes in it

8 oz (200 g) cottage cheese
5 oz (125 g) natural yoghurt
$^1/_2$ red pepper
$^1/_2$ green pepper
1 tbs chopped chives
$^1/_4$ tsp french mustard
salt and pepper

How to make

1. Sieve the cottage cheese into a bowl by pushing it through the sieve with the back of a spoon.
2. Stir in the yoghurt.
3. Chop the peppers into small cubes and add them with the other ingredients to the cottage cheese and stir well.

Then Lucie thought of something else she could make with Mr McGregor's garden vegetables.

MR McGREGOR'S CABBAGE AND CARROT COLESLAW

What goes in it - for 4 people

¹/₂ white cabbage
3 large carrots, scraped
5 oz (125 g) mayonnaise
3oz (75 g) natural yoghurt
1 oz (25 g) raisins

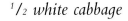

How to make

1. Shred the cabbage into very fine strips with a sharp knife on a chopping board and put in a bowl.
2. Grate the carrots on the largest hole size of your grater and mix with the cabbage.
3. In a separate bowl, mix the mayonnaise with the yoghurt and then pour over the cabbage and carrots and mix it all in.
4. Stir in the raisins.

Next, Lucie thought about Flopsy, Mopsy and Cotton-tail. 'I know they like blackberries,' she said. 'I saw them picking some down the lane. I'll make them a blackberry pudding.' Lucie added another recipe to her list:

FLOPSY, MOPSY AND COTTON-TAIL'S
BLACKBERRY PUDDING

**What goes in it
– for 4 people**

*1 lb (450 g) blackberries
5 oz (125 g) natural yoghurt
10 oz (250 g) Greek yoghurt
4 tbsp dark soft brown sugar*

How to make

1. Wash the blackberries and put them in a bowl.

2. Mix the two yoghurts together in a separate bowl with a spoon and pour over the blackberries.

3. Sprinkle the sugar over the yoghurt and put in the fridge to chill for about half an hour so that the sugar dissolves into the yoghurt and blackberry mixture.

Note: you can make this pudding using raspberries, blueberries or other soft fruit.

'Now, what about Mrs Rabbit?' Lucie asked. 'What does she like to eat?'

Mrs Tiggy-winkle, who was ironing Mrs Rabbit's handkerchief, said she thought Mrs Rabbit liked onions because her handkerchief did so smell of them before she washed it. 'But if you please'm, I don't think Peter and his cousin Benjamin would like onions. It was while they were carrying onions in Mrs Rabbit's hanky as a present for her that they met a cat and had to hide under a basket for *five* hours and the onions made them cry.'

'No, I don't like onions either,' said Lucie. 'They make me cry too. But I could make some cat-shaped biscuits to remind Peter and Benjamin of their adventures.'

BENJAMIN BUNNY'S BISCUITS

What goes in them - for about 10 biscuits

4 oz (100 g) soft butter
2oz (50 g) caster sugar
8 oz (200 g) plain flour
pinch of salt

How to make

1. Turn the oven on to 325°F/160°C/gas mark 3.
2. Put the butter in a bowl with the sugar and beat it with a wooden spoon until the mixture is white and fluffy and the sugar doesn't feel gritty.
3. Sieve the flour and salt into the mixture and stir well.
4. Lightly flour a large wooden chopping board and a rolling pin and roll the mixture out until it is 5 mm ($^1/_4$ inch) thick.
5. Using a round shaped cutter, press out 10 shapes or as many as you can and put onto some greaseproof paper on a baking tray.
6. Mark a cat face onto each biscuit using a knife. At the top, mark two upside-down Vs for ears, then prick two holes for eyes. Below the eyes mark an upside-down triangle as a nose and on either side of the nose score lines for whiskers.
7. Put in the oven and bake for 25-30 minutes or until golden brown.
8. Put the biscuits onto a wire rack to cool before eating.

Mrs Tiggy-winkle had finished her ironing. 'If you please'm, I think we should now have a cup of tea. After tea we will give Peter Rabbit's friends their nice, clean clothes and you can ask them what they like to eat.' And Mrs Tiggy-winkle busied herself with a kettle.

'Are you making camomile tea, like Mrs Rabbit?'

'Oh no'm, this is blackcurrant tea. It's very refreshing after hot ironing, and easy to make. And I also have some lemonade which I'll tell you how to make.'

MRS TIGGY-WINKLE'S
REFRESHING TEA-TIME DRINKS

BLACKCURRANT TEA
What goes in it – for 2 large cups
2 tbsp blackcurrant jam or jelly
2 slices lemon
1 pint (600 ml) boiling water

How to make

1. Put the jam or jelly into a jug with the slices of lemon.

2. Boil some water in a kettle and measure out 1 pint carefully into a measuring-jug.

3. Pour this water into the jug with the jam and stir well. If you drink it while it's hot, drink it in small sips. But it's good cold too.

LEMONADE
What goes in it – for 4 tall glasses

4 lemons

4 oz (100 g) caster sugar

2 pints (1 litre) boiling water

How to make

1. Peel the lemons thinly with a small knife and put the rind in a jug with the sugar.

2. Boil some water in a kettle and measure out 2 pints. Pour the water into a jug with the lemon rind and stir with a spoon until the sugar dissolves. Leave until it is cold.

3. Strain the lemon water through a sieve into another jug and then squeeze the juice from the lemons into the water and stir with a spoon.

5. Put ice into 4 glasses and fill with the lemonade.

When Lucie and Mrs Tiggy-winkle had finished tea, they tied up the clothes in bundles, came out and locked the door and hid the key under the door-sill.

They began to walk down the hill when Lucie suddenly stopped. In the distance, over the hill and far away, she could see what looked like two pigs. They were holding hands and dancing. 'If you please' m, that's Pigling Bland and Pig-wig,' said Mrs Tiggy-winkle. 'I'm sure they would love to come to the party. I believe that Pig-wig is very fond of peppermints.'

Lucie added them to her party food list.

PEPPERMINTS FOR PIG-WIG

What goes in them
– for 24 peppermints
1lb (450 g) icing sugar
2 tbsp double cream
1 egg white
peppermint essence

How to make

1. Put the icing sugar into a bowl with the cream and mix to a paste, smoothing out any lumps with the back of a spoon.

2. Crack the egg open into a wide saucer carefully so that you don't break the yolk. Put an egg cup over the yolk and then tilt the saucer over the bowl with the icing sugar so that only the egg white goes in.

3. Stir the egg white into the icing sugar paste and then add 6 drops of peppermint essence and stir them in as well.

4. Sprinkle some icing sugar onto greaseproof paper and roll the peppermint paste out on this until it is about 1 cm ($^1/_2$ inch) thick. Cut into squares and leave overnight to dry out before eating.

'Does Pigling Bland like peppermints too?' asked Lucie.

'Oh yes, miss. But I think he prefers porridge oats.'

Lucie thought that porridge wasn't very suitable for a party, but then she had an idea and wrote down:

PIGLING BLAND'S PORRIDGE OATS FLAPJACKS

What goes in them
– for about 24 biscuits

4 oz (100 g) margarine

3tbs golden syrup

3 oz (75 g) dark soft brown sugar

8 oz (200 g) rolled porridge oats

2 oz (50 g) chopped hazelnuts.

How to make

1. Turn the oven on to 350°F/180°C/ gas mark 4.

2. Melt the margarine with the golden syrup and sugar in a pan over a low heat.

3. Stir in the oats and the chopped nuts and mix well.

4. Rub a bit of margarine on a 18 x 28 cm (7 x 11 inch) shallow tin and spoon the mixture in, smoothing the top with a palette knife.

5. Bake in the oven for 25-30 minutes.

6. Cool in the tin for a couple of minutes before cutting into squares. Cool completely before taking the flapjacks out of the tin.

Lucie and Mrs Tiggy-winkle continued to walk down the hill until they came to a little damp house amongst the buttercups at the edge of a pond. Outside it was Mr Jeremy Fisher. Mrs Tiggy-winkle gave him his clothes, all neatly washed and ironed.

'Very good of you, Mrs Tiggy-winkle. Very good of you, indeed,' said Mr Jeremy Fisher. 'I'm afraid I have some more washing for you too,' he said, and handed her another parcel of clothes 'Don't know how things get dirty so quickly.' Then, looking at Lucie, he asked, 'And who's this with you? I don't believe we've met.'

'I'm Lucie,' said Lucie. 'And I'm having a party for Peter Rabbit's birthday. I'm asking all his friends to come. But I need to know what everybody likes to eat so everyone is happy. Would you like to come?'

'Jolly good of you to ask, my dear. Be delighted. And since you ask, I must say I rather like fish m'self when I can catch'em. Very tricky, don't you know. Nearly had a fatal accident with a trout only this afternoon. That's why me fingers have got plasters on them.'

'Oh, poor you,' said Lucie. 'Well, I'll make you some fish fingers.'

MR JEREMY FISHER'S
FISH FINGERS

What goes in them – for 20 fingers

¹/₂ lb (250 g) potatoes

knob of butter

3 tbs milk

10 oz (250 g) tin of salmon or fresh cooked salmon

¹/₂ tsp salt and pepper

1 tsp parsley

2 slices brown bread, crumbled into breadcrumbs

1 heaped tbs flour

2 tbs (approx.) vegetable oil

How to make

1. Peel the potatoes with a vegetable peeler and then cut them in half. Put them in a saucepan with enough water to cover them and boil for about 15–20 minutes until the potatoes are soft enough for a knife to go through them easily.

2. Drain the potatoes. Put them in a bowl with the butter and milk and mash them with a fork or potato masher. It doesn't matter if they're a bit lumpy.

3. Flake the fish into the potatoes (if you're using fresh salmon make sure you've removed all the bones). Add salt and pepper.

4. Cut the stalks off the parsley, chop the leaves finely and add to the fish with the breadcrumbs, mixing them in well.

5. Flatten the fish mixture on a board until it's about 2 cm (^{3}/$_4$ inch) thick and cut into finger shapes.

6. Sprinkle the flour on to a plate and coat the fingers with flour on both sides.

7. Heat the oil in a frying pan and add the fish fingers. You probably won't be able to fit all the fish fingers in the pan at the same time so just cook a few at a time. Cook for 4 minutes on either side and keep the first ones hot in an oven while you cook the rest.

6. Drain them on kitchen paper before eating.

'I say, those sound awfully good. Don't want to put you to any trouble, though. If sandwiches are easier, I don't deny I'm rather partial to them too.'

'Oh, of course. Everybody likes sandwiches. I can make lots of different ones.' So Lucie sat down and made a note of some interesting things she could put in sandwiches:

MR JEREMY FISHER'S SANDWICH FILLINGS

* cream cheese and redcurrant jelly
* hardboiled egg cut into slices with cress and mayonnaise
* banana and honey
* tuna fish mixed with salad cream and lettuce
* grated cheddar cheese, tomato and pickle
* sliced cucumber and yeast extract
* peanut butter and banana

PITTA POCKET SANDWICHES

What goes in them – for 2 sandwiches

1 pitta bread
4 lettuce leaves
$^1/_2$ cucumber
1 tomato
2 oz (50 g) feta cheese or similar goat's cheese

How to make

1. Cut the pitta bread in two and open each half to make a pocket.
2. Tear the lettuce leaves into small bits and put inside the two pockets.
3. Chop the cucumber, tomato and cheese into bite-sized cubes and use to fill your pitta pockets.

Lucie finished writing down the things she would need to make sandwiches and then said she thought they ought to be going. She had some more people to invite.

'Well, I'll look forward to the party,' said Mr Jeremy Fisher. 'S'pose I'd better be doing some cooking m'self. I've asked my friends Mr Alderman Ptolemy Tortoise and Sir Isaac Newton to dinner. Can't offer them any minnows but I don't suppose the Alderman will mind. He only likes salad. P'raps I'll make them roasted grasshopper with ladybird sauce. That's always a favourite.'

'How horrid,' thought Lucie, but she said, 'I don't think I could quite make that. But if your friends would like to come to Peter Rabbit's party, I'll make a lovely salad.'

Mr Jeremy Fisher thanked them both. He felt sure that his friends would be honoured to attend a party for Peter Rabbit and that a salad would be much appreciated. Lucie added to her list:

ALDERMAN PTOLEMY TORTOISE'S SALAD

**What goes in it
- for 4-6 people**

1 gem lettuce

10 spinach leaves

$1/2$ cucumber

7 oz (175 g) tin sweet corn

4 oz (100 g) frozen peas, thawed

4 oz (100 g) hard cheese

6 cherry tomatoes

Dressing

3 tbsp salad oil

1 tbsp white wine vinegar

$1/2$ tsp sugar

1 tsp French mustard

salt and pepper

1. Chop the stalk off the bottom of the lettuce, divide the leaves and wash with the spinach in cold water. Drain and pat the leaves dry with a clean tea-towel or kitchen paper. Put them in a large bowl.

2. Peel the cucumber with a vegetable peeler and cut into thin slices, and add to the bowl.

3. Drain the sweet corn and tip into the salad bowl with the peas.

4. Cut the cheese into 1 cm ($1/2$ inch) cubes and place in the middle of the salad.

5. Slice the tomatoes and arrange round the side of the salad bowl.

For the dressing: Put all the ingredients in a jar with a screw top. Shake it so everything is well mixed up and pour over the salad.

The next house Lucie and Mrs Tiggy-winkle visited belonged to Mrs Tabitha Twitchit. Her three kittens, Moppet, Mittens and Tom Kitten were tumbling about the doorstep as usual, playing in the dust, and Mrs Tabitha was in the kitchen. It was baking day and she had just finished taking some scones out of the oven.

'Those look good,' said Lucie. 'Will you tell me how to make them?' And Lucie explained about the party for Peter Rabbit.

MRS TABITHA TWITCHIT'S SCONES

What goes in them

8 oz (200 g) self-raising flour
1 tsp salt
2 oz (50 g) margarine
1 oz (25 g) sugar
1/4 pint (600 ml) milk

How to make

1. Turn the oven to 450°F/230°C/gas mark 7.
2. Sieve the flour and salt into a large bowl.
3. Cut the margarine into small pieces and rub into the flour with

the tips of your fingers until the mixture looks like fine breadcrumbs. Then add the sugar and stir it in.

4. Pour most of the milk in and stir to make a soft dough. It should feel a bit sticky, so if it doesn't, add the rest of the milk.

5. Lightly flour a rolling pin and pastry board and roll out the dough until it is about 1 cm ($^1/_2$ inch) thick.

6. Using a round-shaped biscuit cutter cut out as many rounds as you can and place on a greased baking sheet.

7. Brush each scone with a little milk before putting in the oven for 10-12 minutes. These are nicest eaten while they're still warm.

35

'You will come to the party, won't you?' asked Lucie when she had finished writing down the recipe.

Mrs Tabitha Twitchit was rather agitated. 'Oh dear, oh dear. The kittens have nothing suitable to wear to a party. They did have such beautiful, elegant clothes which I always made them wear for my tea parties, but at the last one those naughty kittens gave their clothes to the Puddle-ducks.'

Lucie said she didn't think it mattered what the kittens wore.

'Well, that's very kind of you. I can't leave the kittens alone for a minute without them getting into some mischief or other. Only the other day Tom Kitten nearly got made into a roly-poly pudding by Samuel Whiskers and Anna Maria. I have had such trouble with those rats.'

After waving goodbye, Lucie and Mrs Tiggy-winkle went off towards the farmyard. They passed Farmer Potatoes' barn and Lucie wondered if she would see Samuel Whiskers and Anna Maria. 'Poor old Tom Kitten. I don't expect he would be very happy if I invited *them* to the party. But do you think he would mind if I made some sausage rolls? They are so good and easy to make. And they're not quite the same thing as roly-poly pudding.'

Mrs Tiggy-winkle thought that Tom Kitten wouldn't mind so Lucie added them to her list as she was walking.

SAMUEL WHISKERS' ROLY-POLY SAUSAGES

What goes in them – for 8 sausage rolls

7 ¹/₂ oz (175 g) packet puff pastry
¹/₂ lb skinless chipolata sausages
milk for glazing

How to make

1. Turn the oven to 400°F/200°C/gas mark 6.
2. Sprinkle a little flour onto a pastry board.

3. Roll out the pastry with a rolling-pin until it is about 25 cms (10 inches) square.

4. Trim round the edges with a sharp knife. Cut the pastry down the middle and across into eight strips 6 cms (2 $\frac{1}{2}$ inches) wide and 12 cms (5 inches) long.

5. Put a sausage at the longest side of each pastry strip and roll it up, pressing the ends down firmly with your finger and thumb.

5. Brush each sausage roll with milk and make two small holes on top of each one with a knife, to let the steam escape during cooking. Put on a greased baking tray with the outer pastry edge turned to the bottom.

6. Bake in the oven for 30 minutes. These are delicious eaten hot or cold.

Lucie and Mrs Tiggy-winkle had reached the farmyard. They could see Jemima Puddle-duck with her sister-in-law, Mrs Rebeccah.

Jemima was very pleased to be asked to Peter Rabbit's party. She would wear her shawl, so beautifully cleaned by Mrs Tiggy-winkle, and her best blue poke bonnet.

'And please, Mrs Puddle-duck,' said Lucie, 'would you be so very kind as to let me have some of your beautiful eggs? I'm going to make a special picnic omelette which I will name after you.'

JEMIMA PUDDLE-DUCK'S PICNIC OMELETTE

What goes in it
– for 4 people

6 eggs

3 tbsps milk

salt and pepper

$^1/_2$ red pepper

$^1/_2$ green pepper

2 new potatoes, cooked

1 oz (25 g) butter

1 oz (25 g) cheddar cheese

How to make

1. Crack the eggs into a bowl and whisk with a fork. Add the milk and a pinch of salt and pepper and stir them in too.

2. Chop the red and green peppers into 5 mm ($^1/_4$ inch) pieces and the cooked potatoes into 1 cm ($^1/_2$ inch) pieces.

3. Heat the butter gently in a large frying pan and when it has melted, add the vegetables. Let the vegetables cook for about 2

minutes and keep turning them so that they don't get burnt.

4. Turn the heat up a little and pour the eggs into the pan. Let the eggs cook without stirring for about 3 minutes. It is ready when the underside looks golden brown. (Check by lifting up an edge with a knife).

5. Grate the cheese over the top of the omelette and then put the frying pan under a hot grill for a minute until the cheese has melted and the egg is set.

6. This can be eaten hot but is very good cold too.

'An omelette named after me! I would be only too glad to be of help,' said Jemima, ruffling her feathers. 'Of course,' she continued proudly, 'the farmer's wife now permits me to hatch my own eggs, but I'm sure I can spare a few.'

The light was beginning to fade. Mrs Tiggy-winkle had given all the clothes back to their owners and she thought it was time she hurried home. Lucie thought she ought to be going home too. She had a lot to do for the party. She thanked Mrs Tiggy-winkle for all her help and, carrying the eggs carefully wrapped in her apron, started to walk back. She thought about all the friends of Peter Rabbit she had met and the things she was going to make. It would be a lovely party and everybody would have something they liked to eat. But there was just one more thing she would have to cook to make a proper party. A cake, and she knew just the cake that Peter would like best.

PETER RABBIT'S PARTY
CARROT CAKE

What goes in it - makes a 20-cm (8-inch) round cake

4 oz (100 g) butter

2 tbsp vegetable oil

8 oz (200 g) carrot

2 apples

6 oz (150 g) soft brown sugar

2 eggs

7 oz (175 g) self-raising flour

3 level tsps baking powder

1 level tsp ground cinnamon

$^1/_2$ tsp salt

4 oz (100 g) raisins

2 oz (50 g) chopped walnuts

3 tbsps milk

Icing

2 oz (50 g) icing sugar

8 oz (200 g) cream cheese

1 tbsp lemon juice

42

How to make

1. Turn the oven on to 350°F/180°C/gas mark 4.

2. Put the butter and oil in a saucepan and heat gently until the butter has melted and then pour into a large bowl.

3. Peel and grate the carrots and apples using the small-sized hole of your grater and beat them into the butter mixture with the sugar and eggs.

4. Sieve the flour, baking powder, cinnamon and salt into the bowl and then add the raisins, walnuts and milk. Mix them all together.

5. Grease a 20-cm (8-inch) round cake tin with a little bit of margarine and then pour the cake mixture into it, scraping all round the sides of the bowl with a spatula so all the cake mixture goes in!

6. Put the tin in the oven and bake for an hour. (One way of checking that the cake is cooked is to put a sharp knife in the middle of it and if the knife comes out clean that means the cake is ready).

7. Leave the cake in the tin for a few minutes before turning it out onto a wire rack to cool. When it is completely cool, carefully cut the cake in half horizontally, ready for the icing.

The Icing

Sieve the icing sugar into a bowl and then beat in the cream cheese and lemon juice. Spread some of the icing on one half of the cake and top with the other half. Spread the rest of the icing on the top of the cake.

INDEX